Is It Our Job to Protect the ENVIRONMENT?

By David Anthony

KidHaven PUBLISHING

Published in 2019 by
KidHaven Publishing, an Imprint of Greenhaven Publishing, LLC
353 3rd Avenue
Suite 255
New York, NY 10010

Designer: Deanna Paternostro
Editor: Katie Kawa

Photo credits: Cover Steve Debenport/E+/Getty Images; p. 5 (top) Syda Productions/ Shutterstock.com; p. 5 (bottom) Rich Carey/Shutterstock.com; p. 7 Nicole S Glass/ Shutterstock.com; p. 9 (top) Ritesh Chaudhary/Shutterstock.com; p. 9 (bottom) Oleg Senkov/ Shutterstock.com; p. 10 Nickolay Khoroshkov/Shutterstock.com; pp. 11 (top), 19 Rawpixel.com/ Shutterstock.com; p. 11 (bottom) Marten_House/Shutterstock.com; p. 12 MCT/Contributor/Tribune News Service/Getty Images; p. 13 (top) Mark Agnor/Shutterstock.com; p. 13 (bottom) franco lucato/ Shutterstock.com; p. 15 testing/Shutterstock.com; p. 17 Chip Somodevilla/Staff/Getty Images News/ Getty Images; p. 21 (notepad) ESB Professional/Shutterstock.com; p. 21 (markers) Kucher Serhii/ Shutterstock.com; p. 21 (photo frame) FARBAI/iStock/Thinkstock; p. 21 (inset, left) Kaichankava Larysa/Shutterstock.com; p. 21 (inset, middle-left) Marianna Ianovska/Shutterstock.com; p. 21 (inset, middle-right) wavebreakmedia/Shutterstock.com; p. 21 (inset, right) A3pfamily/ Shutterstock.com.

Cataloging-in-Publication Data

Names: Anthony, David.
Title: Is it our job to protect the environment? / David Anthony.
Description: New York : KidHaven Publishing, 2019. | Series: Points of view | Includes glossary and index.
Identifiers: ISBN 9781534525726 (pbk.) | 9781534525719 (library bound) | ISBN 9781534525733 (6 pack) | ISBN 9781534525740 (ebook)
Subjects: LCSH: Environmental protection–Juvenile literature. | Environmental degradation–Prevention–Juvenile literature. | Environmental quality–Juvenile literature.
Classification: LCC QE511.A58 2019 | DDC 363.7–dc23

Printed in the United States of America

CPSIA compliance information: Batch #BS18KL: For further information contact Greenhaven Publishing LLC, New York, New York at 1-844-317-7404.

Changing the
PLANET

The natural world—also known as the environment—is always changing, and people play a big part in causing those changes. People change the environment in a negative, or bad, way when they pollute the air or water or cut down trees. However, they can change the environment for the better when they work to protect it, or keep it safe.

Many people believe it's our job to protect the environment because people are the creatures who have done the most harm to Earth. Others believe people shouldn't have to change their lives to protect the **planet**.

Know the Facts!

In a 2016 study, 20 percent of Americans said they try to help protect the environment all the time.

The different points of view people have about protecting the environment **affect** how they treat the planet. Keep reading to learn more about why people have these different opinions and to help you form your own.

One part of Earth that's changing because of human activity is its climate, or the weather in a place over a long period of time. Scientists have discovered that gases put into the air by people are causing the planet to get warmer, which is making the climate change in places around the world.

As Earth gets warmer, ice starts to melt, which puts more water in the oceans. This can cause flooding. Climate change also causes many other problems, but some people don't believe it's our job to stop it.

Know the Facts!

Since the late 1800s, Earth's average temperature has gone up about 2 degrees Fahrenheit (1.1 degrees Celsius).

Global warming is the term scientists use for the fact that Earth is getting hotter. Many people are working to stop this from happening, but others believe global warming isn't a problem people should worry about.

A Natural
PROCESS

People who aren't worried about global warming often argue that Earth has gone through periods of climate change many times before. At different times in Earth's history, much of the planet was covered with ice. These periods were called ice ages. After an ice age, the planet would go through a period of warming.

Because climate change has happened naturally before, some people believe what's going on now is **normal** for the planet. They don't think there's any reason to try to stop what they see as part of a natural cycle of warming and cooling.

Know the Facts!

Glaciers are large bodies of slowly moving ice. Scientists study them to learn more about climate change in the past and present.

Some people believe it's not our job to try to save glaciers from melting because it's a natural **process**.

People Are the
PROBLEM

Periods of climate change have happened before, but most scientists believe the one happening now is different. It's happening much more quickly than it has in the past. Also, most scientists believe the planet is warming so quickly because of human activity.

This is the first period of global climate change in history that has been most likely caused by people. Because people are the main cause of the problem, many believe people should also try to fix it by reducing the amount of air pollution.

Know the Facts!

Greenhouse gases are gases people put into the air that trap the sun's warmth on Earth, which makes the planet hotter. Greenhouse gases are often put into the air by burning **fossil fuels**, such as coal and oil.

Cutting down trees can make climate change worse because trees take in some greenhouse gases that harm the planet. Some people believe we should stop cutting down trees and should plant new ones to protect the environment.

Too Much Money, Not Enough
JOBS

Protecting the environment costs money. New cars that create less air pollution and changes to factories to burn fewer fossil fuels can be expensive. Some people feel it's not fair to ask people and businesses to spend a lot of money to protect the planet.

In some cases, people also worry that taking care of the environment could become more important than making sure people have jobs. For example, some people who work with coal or oil could lose their jobs if the use of fossil fuels is reduced.

Know the Facts!

The Environmental Protection Agency (EPA) is the part of the U.S. government that is in charge of keeping Earth and the people who live on it healthy.

Some people think protecting the environment shouldn't be more important than protecting people's jobs. Other people, however, believe new jobs can be created in fields in that are working to protect the environment.

SICK

People who believe it's our job to protect the environment believe this helps all living things. We should work to keep the planet healthy because that keeps people healthy.

Studies have shown that pollution can make people very sick. Dirty water causes many different diseases, or illnesses. Also, the World Health Organization (WHO)—a group that works to improve health around the world—has stated that reducing air pollution would reduce cases of heart disease, **lung cancer**, and other sicknesses.

Know the Facts!

According to the WHO, 7 million people died in 2012 because of health problems connected to air pollution.

In some parts of the world, the air pollution is so harmful that people are told to wear masks to protect themselves from it.

Free to
CHOOSE

Most people agree that protecting the environment is important. However, not everyone agrees about how it should be done.

Some leaders believe the best way to protect the environment is to pass laws to reduce pollution and keep animals and plants safe. However, there are people who don't like these laws. They think the government shouldn't tell them what to do. Many of these people support protecting the environment, but they don't want to be forced to do it. They believe people should have the freedom to choose to help the planet.

Know the Facts!

Almost half of Americans in a 2017 study said they believe it's possible to cut back on environmental **regulations** and still protect the air and water.

Even presidents can have different points of view about protecting the environment! When Barack Obama (right) was president of the United States, many regulations were created to reduce the use of fossil fuels. However, when Donald Trump (left) became president, he stated that he wanted to remove many of these regulations.

Earth Is Our
HOME

People who work to protect the environment often state that they're doing so for the people who will live on Earth after them. They want those people to live on a clean and healthy planet.

Earth is our home, and there's only one of it. This is why many people believe it's so important to take care of it. They compare it to keeping your room clean because it's where you live. If you make a mess in your room, it's often your job to clean it up. Many people believe it works the same way with the planet.

Know the Facts!

According to a 2016 study, 74 percent of Americans support doing whatever it takes to protect the environment.

There are many ways to help the environment. If you believe it's our job to protect the planet, it's easy to get started!

An Educated
OPINION

For many years, people didn't understand how much they could affect the environment. Now, though, scientists have shown us how much our actions can help and hurt the planet we call home. With this new understanding, the belief that we need to protect the environment has grown. However, there are some people who use different facts to back up different points of view about protecting the environment.

After learning about these different points of view, what do you think? Is it our job to protect the environment?

Know the Facts!

More than nine out of ten scientists agree that people are the main cause of global warming.

Is it **our job** to **protect** the **environment?**

YES

- Scientists believe humans are causing Earth's climate to change more quickly than ever before.

- Protecting the environment can keep people healthier and save lives.

- When people make a mess where they live, it's their job to clean it up.

- The people who live on Earth after us should be able to live on a clean planet.

NO

- Periods of climate change have happened throughout Earth's history without people playing a part.

- Protecting the environment can cause people to lose their jobs.

- Protecting the environment can cost money people don't have.

- Protecting the environment should be something people choose to do—not something they feel they have to do.

Using this chart and the facts you learned as you read, you can form your own educated, or informed, opinion about protecting the environment.

21

GLOSSARY

affect: To produce an effect on something.

fossil fuel: A fuel, such as coal, oil, or natural gas, that is formed in the earth from dead plants or animals.

global: Relating to the whole world.

lung cancer: A sometimes deadly sickness in which cells grow in the body parts that are used to breathe air in ways they should not.

normal: Usual.

planet: A large body that moves around a star such as the sun.

process: A series of actions or changes.

regulation: A rule or law telling how something is to be done.

INFORMATION

WEBSITES

NASA: Climate Kids
climatekids.nasa.gov
This website allows visitors to learn more about climate change and the ways people can help fight against it.

ZOOM Into Action: You Can Help the Environment!
pbskids.org/zoom/activities/action/way04.html
If you're interested in doing your part to protect the environment, this website has many different activities to help you get started.

BOOKS

Hunt, Jilly. *Protecting Our Planet.* Chicago, IL: Heinemann-Raintree, 2018.

Sawyer, Ava. *Humans and Earth's Atmosphere: What's in the Air?* North Mankato, MN: Capstone Press, 2018.

Sherman, Jill. *Fossil Fuels.* New York, NY: Enslow Publishing, 2018.

INDEX